KNOW AND DEAL WITH A NARCISSIST

Steps to deal with a self-important person, a narcissistic mother, father, husband, and friend and how to heal and recover from them.

Patience John

This book is a work of non-fiction. The names, characters, places, and incidents are products of the author's imagination or are used fictitiously. Any resemblance to actual events, locales, or persons, living or dead, is entirely coincidental.

TABLE OF CONTENT

INTRODUCTION

She first met him at a crowded coffee shop on a rainy afternoon. He had a charming smile that seemed to light up the room, and his confidence was magnetic. He approached her with smooth words and genuine interest—or so she thought.

"Hi there, I couldn't help but notice you sitting here. Mind if I join you?" he asked, his voice warm and inviting.

They had a great and heartfelt conversation, no doubt. Without a stitch in time, they both seemed to have gotten to know each other so well and just desire for more.

"He looks so handsome, a great gentleman indeed. Who wouldn't want a gentle and charismatic man as a potential husband?" she kept staring at him with admiration while running through her day-dreaming thoughts.

They started seeing each other more often, and his excessive sweet words seemed more inviting, calling her into a relationship she probably was expecting and dreaming of. Their conversations were always captivating: they seemed to have plenty to talk about and how to talk about it, except that some compliments were careless insults.

"You look so pretty even with your protruding stomach," he once said on one of their dates, aiming to admire or, should I say, insult her. He had a way of making her feel special, like she was the most important person in the world… that she blushed on.

"I love hearing about your day. Tell me more," he'd say each time during their conversation, leaning in with genuine curiosity.

As their relationship progressed, she couldn't help but feel lucky to have found someone so charming and attentive. He would surprise her with thoughtful gestures and lavish gifts, always making her feel like she was living in a fairy tale.

But slowly, subtle signs began to reveal themselves.

One of those days, he had invited her to his friend's party in Las Vegas.

"Please don't dress too flamboyantly for the party, look as simple as possible, it's nothing serious," she agreed, even though she was tempted to ask why he was putting on a suit and tie if it wasn't serious. But I guess she didn't want to pull up another fight and argument, which she never had a winning chance because he would end up making her take the blame while he played the victim.

On getting there, he left her in the car and rushed into the friend's party venue as it was beginning to snow. She walked into the party hall to find out that she dressed the least of everyone invited; both the ladies and the men didn't look anything close to ordinary. To be honest, it was a big occasion hosted by one of the prominent men in society. But there she was, looking like a maid with her long dress and a scarf to match and nothing of good suitable makeup… Well, it would've been better if she had styled it, but at this point, she seemed to be at the mercy of someone, unknowingly to her.

She weaved her way to a suitable spot where she could not be noticed and possibly hide from the women who looked classier than she was… So she reasoned.

She sighted him with his friends, laughing, conversing, exchanging pleasantries, and sipping wine… Oops! She didn't even get noticed or proudly introduced by her own man. After some moments had passed, he walked to her with one of his friends and came bragging and bragging about how much he got his suit for.

At this moment, she was more than embarrassed to give a response… *"Why would you bring me to this place looking like a homeless child, someone without class?"* she kept wondering in her thoughts.

Suddenly, he sat right by her and pulled her close in front of his friend and said, "You know, I always get compliments on my looks, so I had to show up looking the best of them all," he mentioned casually, a hint of arrogance in his tone.

She brushed off these behaviours at first, attributing them to his confidence and strong personality.

Not after she witnessed him kissing and snuggling with another woman in the crowd. I guess she had witnessed enough of his behaviour so she stepped out and went to wait for him by his car; she was boiling inside with anger ready to explode on him without any restraint this time. She waited and got tired until a few hours later and was beginning to feel tired and weary and thus reposed herself on the car bumper and dozed off, only to wake up to meet her man with the same woman in the act.

"Brain, does it ever occur to you that you are directly insulting and embarrassing me in this… Whatever party you brought me to… right in front of me, you are snuggling with another woman with no regard to me at all… What on earth is going on with you, Brain…? Are you crazy? And you, bitch, fuck the hell off my man?" she exploded finally, voicing it all out of her chest.

"That's the problem with you, Tracy, you are always making trouble wherever you go. I did you a great deal to bring you to such a reputable occasion, only for you to curse me and my friend out right now without any respect at all. After all I have done for you to be happy… I see, so this is the reason you came out here without my knowledge, just so you can insult me, is this how ungrateful you are? You know, you should be grateful to have me. Not many people have the opportunity you have. And so what if you find me with another woman, how is that your business, and how does that have anything to do with you?" he spoke as though he was the victim of the whole situation and with superiority in his voice.

At this point, he drove away in his car with the other woman, leaving Tracy dumbfounded and alone in the dark outside the party ground.

She found herself walking on eggshells, afraid to say or do anything that might bruise his delicate ego. She seemed to be caught under his spell.

This wasn't the first time he reminded her of how lucky she was to have him. She flashed her mind back on the last couple of conversations they had.

"I don't think you understand how lucky you are to have me," he had said with a smug smile playing on his lips.

The following day, he apologized; he always apologized whenever he stepped on her toes, and as sincere as the apologies appeared, he kept doing the worst every time. She realized that maybe a talk with someone, a friend, whoever it will be, just so some advice could be given to her.

It wasn't until she confided in a close friend about her concerns that she realized the truth: she was in a relationship with a narcissist.

"He's always making everything about himself. I don't know what to do," she'd admit, her voice trembling with uncertainty.

At first, she struggled to accept the reality of her situation. She had invested so much time and energy into the relationship, hoping that things would change. But deep down, she knew that she deserved better than to be constantly belittled and manipulated.

This book isn't a storybook, but sincerely, that's the reality for many people. Tracy had met a good and endearing man as she thought, probably must have started planning her wedding in her head, not until Brain failed to take responsibility for his actions, raised himself above unreachable class, and placed Tracy where she feels unimportant and insignificant just to be the center of attraction. The truth is, it's easier to mistake a narcissist for a good person because at first, they will try to appear as good, loving, and even charismatic people, someone with the energy you will love to be around. But at the end, the manipulation, gas-lighting, egotism, self-importance, and all other uncalled energy a narcissistic person emits can be very stressful and frustrating to handle.

To survive a narcissistic energy, you must make sure to take their power from their hand, pluck their wings, and reduce them to nothing.

This book will give you all the strategies you need to know and do to achieve this feat.

Each chapter deeply explains what you need to know, how to go about dealing with them, and the nuances involving a narcissist.

CHAPTER 1

Understanding Narcissism

There are those who doesn't know what narcissism means and when that happens they may even be a narcissist themselves not knowing that they are hurting others with their terrible attitude. Whiles others who are dealing with narcissist may also not know that is sometimes attributed to sickness or probably a sickness and thus may blame themselves when a narcissist manipulate or subject them to self-worthlessness or feels there are the problem meanwhile is the other person, not them. We will elaborate first on what a narcissist is.

Narcissism is when someone thinks they're more important than others, always wants attention, and doesn't care much about how others feel. Understanding narcissism means knowing what behaviours show it and how it affects relationships and mental health.

People with narcissistic traits often want others to praise them to feel good about themselves. They might act like they're better than everyone else and expect special treatment. They also might not understand or care about how others feel.

Narcissism isn't all the same; it can range from mild traits to a serious condition called Narcissistic Personality Disorder (NPD). Even mild traits can make relationships hard.

Understanding narcissism means noticing signs like manipulating others, taking advantage of them, and not taking responsibility for their actions. It's also about understanding the reasons behind these behaviours, like feeling insecure deep down.

When we understand narcissism, we can handle relationships with people who show these traits better. It helps us be kinder and more understanding while also knowing when to set boundaries and take care of ourselves.

To help you grab the point. Note that understanding narcissism means recognizing the signs, knowing how it affects relationships and people, and figuring out how to deal with it in a healthy way.

Defining Narcissistic Personality Disorder (NPD)

Narcissistic Personality Disorder (NPD) is when someone feels really important, always wants praise, and doesn't care much about others' feelings. Let's see what this means and how it affects people:

1. **Feeling really important**: People with NPD often think they're better than everyone else. They might brag about how great they are and believe they deserve special treatment. This feeling of being extra special affects how they treat others.

2. **Always Wanting Praise**: People with NPD really want others to think they're awesome. They need constant praise and attention to feel good about themselves. This can

make them act in sneaky ways to make sure others see them as great.

3. **Not Caring about Others**: One big thing about NPD is that people with it don't really care about how others feel. They struggle to understand or care about others' feelings and experiences. They might ignore what others need or how they feel, thinking they're not as important.

NPD can vary from mild to severe, and some people might show only a few traits while others have a full diagnosis.

Diagnosing NPD means a mental health professional looks at how someone acts, thinks, and feels. There's a book called the DSM-5 that explains what traits someone needs for an NPD diagnosis.

Living with NPD can be tough for both the person with it and those around them. It can make relationships hard and affect how they work and live. Treatment often involves therapy to help them understand why they act the way they do and learn better ways to relate to others.

In short, Narcissistic Personality Disorder is when someone feels really important, always wants praise, and doesn't care much about others' feelings. Understanding NPD helps diagnose and treat it better and shows more support and empathy for those dealing with it.

Exploring the Origins and Development of Narcissistic Traits

Welcome to our journey into understanding why people act narcissistic and how it happens. We will now go deep into the complicated reasons behind these traits and how they grow.

Narcissistic traits don't just pop out of nowhere; they have deep roots in our lives. They start from the time we're kids, how our families treat us, what society values, and even our own personalities. Let's break it down:

1. ***Early Life happenings***: What happens to us when we're young really shapes who we become. If we get too much praise or criticism, feel ignored, or get spoiled rotten, it can lead to being narcissistic later on. Kids who don't feel loved consistently might try really hard to get attention when they grow up.

2. ***Family Dynamics***: Our families play a huge role in how we see ourselves and others. In families where being successful is everything or where people don't talk about feelings much, kids might learn to think only about themselves. But in families that care about others and set rules, kids might learn to care more about other people.

3. ***Society's Influence***: What we see and hear every day also affects how we act. In places where being famous or having lots of stuff is all that matters, people might act

more narcissistic. Social media and TV make it seem like being rich and famous is the best thing ever, which makes narcissistic behaviour more common.

4. **Who We are**: Everyone is different, and some people might be more likely to act narcissistic because of who they are. Some people might feel unsure about themselves, which could make them act more narcissistic to feel better.

When you know why people act narcissistic it will help us see that everyone has their own story. It also reminds us to be kind to everyone, even if they act narcissistic. Everyone has their own problems, and being nice can help us all get along better.

Let's learn more about why people act narcissistic and remember to be understanding and friendly to everyone we meet.

Examining the Diagnostic Criteria for Narcissism

Understanding how experts diagnose narcissism is key to recognizing and dealing with this personality trait. Let's break down the specific signs that mental health professionals use to spot narcissistic personality disorder (NPD). Here we are going to categorically list out the behaviours criteria to diagnose a narcissist

1. ***Feeling Extra Important***: People with NPD often act like they're better than everyone else. They might brag about what they've done and think they're superior. This feeling of being extra special is a big part of narcissism and helps doctors identify it.

2. ***Always Wanting Approval***: People with NPD always want others to think they're amazing. They need constant praise and attention to feel good about themselves. This need for approval can make them act in sneaky ways to make sure others like them.

3. **Not Caring About Others**: One major thing about NPD is that people with it don't really care about others' feelings. They struggle to understand or care about how others feel. They might ignore what others need or how they feel because they think they're not as important.

4. **Thinking They Deserve Special Treatment**: People with NPD often think they deserve to be treated better than everyone else. They expect others to do what they want without thinking about how others feel or what they need.

5. **Using Others for Their Own Benefit**: People with NPD might use others to get what they want without feeling bad about it. They might take advantage of others' weaknesses or trick them to help themselves, even if it hurts others.

6. ***Feeling Jealous and Acting Arrogant***: People with NPD might get jealous of others who seem more successful or popular. They might also act like they're better than everyone else, looking down on people they think are beneath them.

7. ***Repeating Patterns of Behaviour***: To diagnose NPD, doctors look for a pattern of acting extra important, always needing praise, and not caring about others' feelings. This behaviour shows up in different situations and over time.

Diagnosing NPD means a doctor carefully looks at how someone acts, thinks, and feels. There's a book called the DSM-5 that explains the specific rules for diagnosing NPD, making sure doctors can diagnose it accurately.

Understanding the Impact of Narcissism on Relationships and Mental Health

At this point, we will really expose some of the negative effect of being or dealing with a narcissist. You will agree with me about some of these effects or it may feel familiar to you probably because you may or someone you know is going through some of these negative effect dealing with a narcissist can cause.

1. **Impact on Relationships**:

- *Unbalanced Dynamics**: When you're in a relationship with a narcissist, things often feel a bit off. They tend to hog the spotlight, always seeking praise, and expecting everyone to revolve around them.

- **_Manipulative Behaviour_**: Narcissists have a knack for manipulation. They might use guilt trips, gas-lighting, or other sneaky tactics to keep things under their control.

- **_Lack of Empathy_**: One tough aspect of dealing with narcissists is their lack of empathy. They often struggle to understand or support others or their partner's feelings, leaving them feeling ignored and alone.

- **_Cycle of Idealization and Devaluation_**: Sometimes, narcissists can swing between adoring you and tearing you down. One moment, they shower you with love, and the next, they're criticizing and belittling you. It's a rollercoaster that can really mess with your heads.

2. **Impact on Mental Health**:

- **Low Self-Esteem**: Being with a narcissist can really chip away at one's self-esteem. Constant criticism and comparisons can make others or their partner feel pretty low.

- **Anxiety and Depression**: Dealing with a narcissist's unpredictable behaviour can lead to anxiety and depression. Always walking on eggshells, fearing criticism or abandonment, really takes a toll on our mental health.

- **Boundary Violations**: What could be worst you can't draw a healthy line to protect yourself from their influence because narcissist often don't respect boundaries. Feeling like your personal space and choices aren't your own can be tough to handle.

- **Isolation and Social Withdrawal**: Sometimes, we might avoid social gatherings because of our partner's behaviour. This isolation can make us feel even more alone and sad.

CHAPTER 2:

Identifying Narcissistic Behaviour Patterns

So far on the previous chapter and headings, we had covered so many trait a narcissistic person has which I believe helps you understand who a narcissist really is.

Seeking attention may be one of those trait that keep ringing in your ear and I am here to assured you that seeking attention isn't bad on itself, and therefore if you put on a beautiful or cloth it's nothing bad seeking a sincere confirmation of your look from someone. A simple 'hello, how do you think I look on this?' doesn't speak of you as a narcissist.

To still pull you back to who a narcissist is, I will categorically list out all the related behaviour pattern of a narcissist once again.

1. **Feeling Super Important**: Narcissists often believe they're better than others and have a big **EGO**.

2. **Craving Attention**: They **CONSTANTLY** seek praise and approval to feel better about themselves.

3. **Missing Empathy**: Understanding others' feelings isn't their strong suit, so they might not get how you're feeling.

4. **Feeling Entitled**: They think they deserve special treatment and expect others to give them what they want without asking nicely.

5. **Playing Tricks**: Sometimes, they might use sneaky moves to control or take advantage of others.

6. **Green with Envy**: They can get jealous of people they think are doing better than them.

7. **Full of Themselves:** They might act all high and mighty because they think they're the best.

8. **Can't Handle Criticism**: Criticism can hurt their feelings, and they might get defensive or blame others.

9. **Using People**: They might use others for their own gain without feeling guilty.

10. **Tricky Relationships**: Because they're so focused on themselves, keeping good relationships can be tough for them.

If you noticed, I bold the main point to take note. Next we will differentiate the difference between narcissism and confidence.

Differentiating Between Healthy Confidence and Narcissism

Mind you, a person may just be confidence and that doesn't mean there are narcissist. How can you know the difference? come with me while we spell out the difference between healthy confidence and narcissism

1. **Understanding Healthy Confidence**:

Healthy confidence stems from a positive self-image and a realistic assessment of one's abilities. Here's what defines healthy confidence:

- Embracing both strengths and weaknesses without exaggeration.

- Feeling comfortable in one's own skin, without constantly seeking validation from others.

- Respecting others' boundaries and perspectives.

- Welcoming feedback as an opportunity for growth.

- Valuing relationships and treating others with kindness and empathy.

2. **Recognizing Narcissistic Traits**:

Narcissism is characterized by an inflated EGO and a lack of empathy. Here are the signs of narcissistic behaviour:

- Exaggerating achievements to maintain a superior self-image.

- Craving constant admiration and validation.

- Demonstrating a lack of empathy towards others' feelings.

- Engaging in manipulative tactics to maintain control.

- Reacting defensively or aggressively to criticism.

3. **Key Differences**:

- Healthy confidence is grounded in authenticity, while narcissism relies on external validation.

- Healthy confidence fosters respectful relationships, while narcissism often leads to a lack of empathy.

- Healthy confidence encourages self-reflection, while narcissism triggers defensive responses to criticism.

- Healthy confidence is based on a realistic self-assessment, while narcissism stems from an inflated sense of self-importance.

Identifying Manipulative Behaviours and Emotional Abuse Tactics

Above many other traits of a narcissist, manipulative behaviour is one of those that can wreak havoc on the mind of the victim. We will highlight the major ways they do so and how you can identify it.

1. **Gas-lighting**

Gas-lighting is a sneaky form of manipulation that makes you doubt your reality. Watch out for these signs:

- When someone denies or downplays your experiences.

- Blaming you for things that aren't your fault.

- Dismissing your feelings or opinions.

- Contradicting themselves to confuse you.

2. **Blame Shifting**

Blame shifting is when someone refuses to own up to their actions and instead blames you. Keep an eye out for:

- Dodging responsibility for their behaviour.

- Making excuses or blaming others for their actions.

- Making you feel guilty for things you didn't do.

- Trying to make you believe you're the problem.

3. **Isolation**

Emotional abusers often try to cut you off from your support network. Look for signs like:

- Discouraging you from seeing friends and family.

- Keeping tabs on your communications and whereabouts.

- Making you feel bad for seeking help outside the relationship.

- Making you feel like you can't function without them.

4. **Manipulative Communication**

Manipulative communication is when someone tries to control you through deceptive tactics. Be aware of:

- Keeping you in the dark or giving you only part of the story.

- Using threats or pressure to get their way.

- Being passive-aggressive or using sarcasm to undermine you.

- Showering you with compliments or charm to get what they want.

5. **Emotional Blackmail**

Emotional blackmail is a powerful tool for controlling others through fear and guilt. Watch out for:

- Threatening to withdraw love or support if you don't comply.

- Using emotional outbursts to manipulate your feelings.

- Making you feel responsible for their happiness.

- Punishing you for asserting yourself or setting boundaries.

Recognizing these manipulative behaviours is the first step toward breaking free from toxic relationships

Exploring the Spectrum of Narcissistic Traits and Behaviours

You will agree with me that when you know the level of a situation and can differentiate it appropriately you will be able to know how to deal with such situation and in the case of a narcissist you will know what level of behaviour can be attribute to NPD or mild narcissism. Here the spectrum to scale the behavioural trait of a narcissist.

1. **Grandiosity vs. Vulnerability**

   - On one side, we have grandiose narcissism, where individuals exhibit an inflated sense of self-importance, craving admiration, and lacking empathy.

   - On the other side, vulnerable narcissism emerges, where individuals grapple with deep feelings of inadequacy and resort to narcissistic behaviours to shield their fragile self-esteem.

2. **Overt vs. Covert Narcissism**

- Overt narcissism displays through overt arrogance, entitlement, and a constant need for attention and validation.

- Covert narcissism, however, manifests in subtler forms like passive-aggressiveness, victimhood, and self-pity, often masked by modesty while still nurturing a sense of entitlement.

3. **Healthy Narcissism vs. Pathological Narcissism**

- Healthy narcissism embodies a balanced self-esteem and self-worth, allowing individuals to express themselves confidently without trampling on others' rights or feelings.

- Pathological narcissism, on the flip side, delves into Narcissistic Personality Disorder (NPD), where narcissistic traits become maladaptive and disruptive, wreaking havoc in relationships and work life.

4. **Adaptive vs. Maladaptive Narcissism**

- Adaptive narcissism involves the strategic use of narcissistic traits in specific situations like leadership roles or competitive environments, leveraging assertiveness and confidence.

- Maladaptive narcissism, however, epitomizes dysfunctional and damaging expressions of narcissistic traits that hinder healthy functioning, leading to conflicts and emotional turmoil.

5. **Situational vs. Chronic Narcissism**

- Situational narcissism arises in response to certain stressors or challenges, prompting individuals to adopt narcissistic behaviours temporarily as a coping mechanism.

- Chronic narcissism encompasses a persistent pattern of narcissistic traits and behaviours that persist over time and across different scenarios, indicating entrenched personality traits and potential personality disorders.

When you know the range of narcissistic traits and behaviours it will helps you differentiate between healthy and harmful expressions of narcissism. This makes it easier to give the right support and interventions. It's also important to consider each person's unique situation and background when identifying narcissistic tendencies. By using this point I highlighted you can increase awareness and empathy in relationships, ultimately enhancing psychological health..

CHAPTER 3

Strategies for Dealing with Narcissists

Dealing with narcissists in relationships can be tough, but there are ways to handle it and protect yourself. Let's explore some strategies together:

1. ***Set Boundaries***

   -Even though a narcissist do not respect boundaries is still essential to establish clear boundaries to shield yourself from manipulation and emotional harm. Be firm and keep your words about what you will and won't tolerate, and stick to your limits.

2. ***Maintain Self-Respect***

   - Hold onto your self-worth and confidence. Remind yourself of your strengths and value, and don't let the narcissist's criticisms get to you.

3. ***Practice Assertive Communication***

- Use assertive communication to express your needs and feelings clearly and confidently. Avoid getting caught up in arguments or power struggles

4. **Avoid Getting into Arguments**

- Refrain from engaging in pointless arguments with the narcissist. Instead, calmly disengage when necessary to avoid unnecessary conflict.

5. **Focus on Self-Care**

- Prioritize activities that nurture your well-being, both physically and emotionally. Spend time doing things you enjoy and surround yourself with supportive people.

6. **Seek Support**

- Reach out to trusted friends, family, or a therapist for support and guidance. Talking to someone who understands can provide comfort and perspective.

7. **Practice Detachment**

- Maintain some distance from the narcissist to protect yourself from their toxic behaviour. Remember that you can't change them, but you can control how you respond.

8. **Stay Empathetic**

- Try to understand the narcissist's insecurities, but don't let their behaviour affect you. It's essential to balance empathy with firm boundaries, don't forget that some narcissist are situational and not chronic and though is worth to say that you should portion out your empathy to them. Some NPD patient as I will address them really needs medical or therapy attention, while others don't even know they are hurting others with their actions. Sadly some may really be battling within just like you are battling from their manipulation.

9. **Limit Contact if Needed**

- If the relationship becomes too toxic, consider reducing or cutting off contact with the narcissist. Your well-being should always come first. If you are married to a narcissist, you may consider separation here isn't divorce because I believe that divorce isn't always the answer. You can try helping them from afar.

10. **Seek Professional Help**

- If you're struggling to cope, consider seeking help from a therapist. They can provide you with coping strategies and support tailored to your situation.

If you follow these strategies, you can navigate relationships with narcissists more effectively while taking care of yourself. Remember, it's okay to prioritize your own well-being in challenging situations. Though a narcissistic person do not respect boundaries but the next sub-heading will focus more on how you can place more emphasis on your boundaries to maintain your personal and mental well-being.

Establishing Boundaries and Asserting Personal Autonomy

As I already tipped you; a narcissist don't seem to respect boundaries yet establishing boundaries and personal autonomy are vital components of maintaining good relationships, particularly when dealing with narcissistic people. Here's a detailed approach on setting limits and asserting your individuality effectively:

1. **Understanding Your Limits**

- Take some time to think about your needs, values, and emotional boundaries. Getting to know what behaviour is acceptable and unacceptable to you is the first step towards setting limits. That way you will better know how to and on what you should give limit on.

2. **Speak clearly**

- Communicate your boundaries clearly and assertively to the other person. Be open and explicit about your needs and expectations in the connection.

3. **Remain Consistent**

- **CONSISTENCY** – I strongly emphasis on this because is essential when it comes to setting limits. Maintain your limits even if the other person attempts to push against them.

Consistency promotes the notion that your limits are non-negotiable.

4. **Practice Self-Care**

- Prioritise self-care activities that promote your physical, emotional, and mental well, don't joke with this aspect. Taking care of yourself allows you to preserve the strength and resilience required to effectively enforce limits.

5. Recognise Manipulative Tactics

- Be aware of the deceptive strategies employed by narcissists to erode your limits. These might involve gaslighting, guilt-tripping, or rejecting your emotions. Maintain your boundaries despite attempts to influence you.

6. ***Establish Your Autonomy***

- Exercise your autonomy by making decisions that reflect your ideals and interests. Take responsibility for your decisions and actions, and don't let others define how you should spend your life.

7. ***Set the Consequences***

- Clearly express the repercussions of crossing your limits. Setting consequences underlines the need of following your boundaries, whether it's by restricting contact, taking a break from the relationship, or seeking outside support.

8. ***Contact Support***

- Surround yourself with a supporting network of friends, family, or a therapist who will verify your limits and offer direction and encouragement as required.

9. **Practise Self-Compassion**

- Be nice to yourself during the process of setting and enforcing limits. It's normal to feel guilty or nervous, but remember that prioritising your own well-being is critical for sustaining positive relationships.

10. **Reassess regularly**

- Reassess your limits on a regular basis to ensure they continue to meet your requirements and ideals. As circumstances change, your limits may need to be adjusted in order to continue performing their intended function efficiently.

Establishing boundaries and claiming personal autonomy allows you to take responsibility of your own well-being while also creating healthier relationships. While it might be difficult as I said, prioritising self-respect and autonomy is recommended for building mutual respect and understanding in whatever relationships you are with a narcissist

Implementing Effective Communication Techniques

If you use an effective communication method when dealing with people who demonstrate narcissistic tendencies you are more likely to keep things in control and better manage situations that occurs. Here's a thorough guide on successful communication in such situations.

1) **Active Listening**

   - Engage in active listening by focusing your whole attention on them and acknowledging their feelings and experiences. Repeat what they've stated to demonstrate comprehension and empathy.

2. **Include "I" statements**

   - Express your ideas, feelings, and concerns using "I" phrases to accept responsibility for your emotions and avoid assigning blame. Say "it breaks my heart when…" rather than "You don't always make me feel…".

3. **Remain Calm and Collected**

- Maintain a cool demeanour and avoid responding rashly to provocations or criticisms. Take a deep breath and wait before answering, giving yourself time to gather your thoughts.

4. **Develop Clear Expectations**

- Communicate your expectations clearly, respectfully, and assertively. Be clear about what you need from the other person and how they can help you.

5. *Avoid Defensiveness*

- Resist the impulse to be defensive or combative, particularly in the face of criticism or allegations. Instead, listen to and try to grasp their point of view.

6. **Practice Empathetic Communication**

- Show empathy and compassion for their feelings and experiences, even if you don't agree with their actions. Recognise and validate their emotions and experiences.

7. **Establish Limits on Negative Behaviour**

- Set limits for harmful behaviours including gas-lighting, manipulation, and verbal abuse. Clearly state that these behaviours are inappropriate and will not be accepted.

8. **Remain Focused on the Issue**

-There is a high tendency to resurrect dead issues probably because it keeps repeating itself or similar, when that happens is will be you adding fuel to a fire you are trying to put off, so keep the talk focused on the current problem at hand and avoid discussing previous grievances or other issues. Address one issue at a time to avoid escalation.

9. **Seeking Common Ground**

- Look for points of agreement or common ground to foster rapport and constructive conversation. Finding common aims or interests might help bridge the divide between opposing ideas.

10. ***Be Patient and Persistent***

- Be patient and persistent in your attempts to communicate properly, particularly if the other person is resistive or defensive. They may need time to grasp and accept your point of view so make sure to persist on communicating and expressing your desires, to help them understand, grasp and come to terms with what you are advocating for.

If you try to implement these excellent communication skills highlighted above, it will help you have better and more constructive encounters with those who display narcissistic qualities. While it may take time and effort, prioritising clear and respectful communication is not to be kick against when it comes to sustaining strong relationships and effectively resolving disagreements. Let's still expand more on this under the next sub-heading

Setting Realistic Expectations and Managing Interactions

Setting realistic expectations and controlling relationships is something to really consider when dealing with a narcissist. Below are the necessary steps you need to take when dealing with a narcissist

Acknowledge the Reality

Recognise that people with narcissistic qualities may struggle to empathise with others and prioritise their needs. Accepting this truth will allow you to set reasonable expectations for your encounters.

Clarify your goals

Clarify your engagement goals before dealing with someone displaying narcissistic behaviour. Determine what you want to accomplish and how you want to feel afterwards.

Set boundaries

Throughout this book, I believe you must have been told about the important of boundaries and why you need to enforce them effectively. Truly, having boundaries and setting them effectively is very important to preserve your well-being and avoid manipulation or emotional abuse. Communicate your limits assertively and consistently, and be prepared to enforce them if necessary.

Manage your expectations

Adjust your expectations to match the realities of the circumstance. Recognise that you may not receive empathy or affirmation from a narcissistic person, and instead focus on your own mental wellness.

Stay grounded

Maintain a sense of reality and avoid becoming swept up in the individual's grandiose or deceptive behaviours. Remind yourself of your own value and ability, regardless of others' affirmation or acceptance.

Practice emotional regulation

Use emotional management skills to control your own feelings and behaviours while interacting with people who display narcissistic qualities. Take slow breaths, concentrate on being cool, and resist being lured into their drama or manipulation.

Use assertive communication.

Use assertive communication skills to convey your wants, preferences, and boundaries with clarity and confidence. Avoid engaging in power battles or emotional manipulation methods.

Be flexible

Maintain a flexible attitude and be open to adjust to the individual's behaviour as needed. Recognise that their reactions and replies may necessitate changes to your communication style or expectations.

Seek Support

Seek help from reliable friends, family members, or a therapist who can provide advice and perspective during difficult situations. Talking to someone who knows the problem might give affirmation and support.

Developing Coping Mechanisms for Emotional Distress and Gas-lighting

Developing coping techniques for emotional discomfort and gaslighting is recommended for anyone navigating relationships with narcissists or others who display similar behaviours. Here's a thorough guide on developing coping techniques to deal with emotional pain and gaslighting:

1. *Recognise Gas-lighting*.

The first step in establishing coping skills is to recognise when gas-lighting is taking place. Gas-lighting is a type of emotional manipulation in which the abuser challenges the victim's reality, leading them to question their perceptions, recollections, and sanity.

2. **Trust Your Instincts**

- Trust your instincts and intuition. Recognise and affirm your feelings if anything feels out of place or does not correspond to your reality. Gas-lighting frequently employs subtle manipulation techniques that might cause you to question your own judgement.

3. **Seeking Validation**

- Seek affirmation from trustworthy friends, family, or a therapist who can provide an objective assessment of the issue. Sharing your experiences with others might help you gain perspective and reinforce your reality.

4. **have a tolerance limit**

- Set clear limits with the person or a narcissist who is participating in gas-lighting behaviours. Communicate your limits assertively and consistently, and be ready to enforce them if they are crossed. Take your tolerance limit very important, because a narcissist will only respect it when you show them that you mean everything about it even the consequences of going against it will surely be carried out.

5. **Maintain Support System**

- Surround yourself with a supporting network of friends, family members, or a therapist who can provide advice, validation, and emotional support during difficult times. Having a support system might make you feel less alone and more capable of dealing with gas-lighting.

6. *Practice Grounding Techniques*

- Use grounding techniques to stay grounded in reality and keep your sense of self in the middle of gas-lighting attempts. Deep breathing, mindfulness, and focusing on your senses may all help you feel grounded and centred.

7 *Journaling**

- Keep a diary to record your ideas, emotions, and experiences. Writing may be a helpful way to process emotions, acquire clarity, uncover patterns of gas-lighting behaviour, relieving you of anxious thought.

8. **Get Professional Help**

- If you're having trouble dealing with gas-lighting or emotional pain, try seeing a therapist or counsellor. A skilled expert may provide you suggestions, support, and validation based on your specific circumstances.

Our next chapter will focus on how you can navigate a relationship with a narcissist.

CHAPTER 4

Navigating Relationships with Narcissists

Navigating relationships with narcissists may be difficult and emotionally demanding because of their deceptive behaviour and lack of empathy. However, with knowledge, understanding, and the appropriate methods, you can reduce conflict and safeguard your well-being. The strategies to dealing with a narcissist are still the same and for a reminder sake and for the sake of emphasis, let's go over it again.

1. **Recognise the Signs**

 -we had outline different signs a narcissist use in dealing with others, it will be beautiful on your part to be attentive to the signs they are showing or dealing with you with, that way you will better know how to tackle it. Look for signs of grandiosity, a persistent desire for adulation, a lack of empathy, and deceptive behaviour.

2. **Have a limit**:

 - Don't ever forget drawing your boundaries to a narcissistic person. I can't count how many times we are talking about this because is absolutely important. When you set limit to the behaviour they shows to you, it will be easier to keep yourself safe from manipulation and emotional abuse. Communicate your boundaries to the narcissist and impose penalties if they are breached.

3. ***Maintain Your Self-Respect***

 - Maintain your self-esteem and don't let the narcissist's behaviour shake your confidence. Remind yourself of your qualities and value, and avoid internalising their critiques or gas. Lighting methods. Have it in mind that, that is who they are and you can't expect the regular treatment you deserve, therefore is essential to maintain your self-respect and not let their negative talks or critics bring you down.

4. **Use Assertive Communication**

- because a narcissist do not care about others feelings, let alone having the ability to listen to others when they try conveying their emotions with mildness, therefore, with that knowledge is recommended that you use aggressive communication skills to convey your wants, preferences, and emotions clearly and forcefully. Avoid becoming involved in power battles or emotional manipulation methods.

5. **Avoid Having Arguments**

- The truth is, when it comes to dealing with a narcissist; yelling, quarrelling, arguments as a whole can never cease. But to protect your peace of mind, avoid being dragged into pointless fights or disagreements with the narcissist. They may thrive on conflict and exploit it as a form of control. Instead, disengage calmly and assertively if needed. When argument is about to begin you can use a statement followed with an immediate action - like 'Please I really don't feel great talking about this, I will like to be excused' then walk away.

6. **Focus on Self-Care**

- Self-care activities are very necessary when dealing with a narcissist. I know we have talked about this several times, but you just can't exclude them in any situation where you are dealing with a narcissist. Whether it's a narcissistic mother, father, brother, relationship partner like a husband, wife, boyfriend, girlfriend, co-workers, and the list is endless.

Imagine being constantly talked down to, belittled, manipulated, blamed, and subjected to other manipulative tactics from a narcissist; all of these can eat away at your mental well-being. Sooner or later, you may also find yourself fighting against becoming a narcissistic person or showing up with that personality just because you are trying to get validation for yourself. This happens because a narcissist has destroyed your mental health, leaving you with self-doubt, self-guilt, and blame.

So when it comes to self-care, don't skimp on it because that will promote your physical, emotional, and mental well. Engage in hobbies, spend time with supportive friends and family, and seek professional assistance as required.

7. **Contact Support**

- You just can't keep quiet and deal with this people alone, so seek help and direction from trusted friends, family, or a therapist. Talking to someone who knows your circumstance might help you get validation and perspective.

8. **Practice Detachment**

- Keep a healthy emotional distance from the narcissist to avoid their harmful behaviour. Remember that you cannot control or alter them; but, you can manage your reaction and how you interact with them.

9. **Remain Empathetic**

- Maintain empathy for the narcissist's underlying concerns and weaknesses, while yet acknowledging that their behaviour is unacceptable. Empathy combined with clear limits is recommended for your well-being.

10. **Limit contact if necessary**

- If the connection becomes toxic or harmful to your mental health, minimise or discontinue communication with the narcissist. Are you dating a narcissist? Break-up from them, married to a narcissist? Separate from them once in a while, living with a narcissist as a family member? Stay away from them, leave home if the need be and relocate. Your well-being should always be your first priority.

11. *Seek Professional Help*

- If you're having trouble coping with a narcissist, consider seeing a therapist or counsellor. They can provide you with methods and assistance that are targeted to your specific circumstances. When it comes to having a listening ear, and someone that is ready to understand you perfectly and look for ways to help you then a professional is who you should consider.

Implementing these tactics will help you handle relationships with narcissists more successfully while prioritising your own well-being and emotional health. Remember that it is OK to set limits and prioritise your needs in these difficult situations. After moving on from a narcissist if the need be, you will need to heal and recover. Let's list it out in the last chapter of this book.

BONUS CHAPTER

Healing and Recovery

If we were to sit in a therapy room and have this conversation with you, trust me, it could take quite some time to conclude. So, to wrap up this topic in this book, I want you to grasp some vital points. Narcissism ranges from mild to severe, and while you may handle their behaviour using this guide, it's advised to take a break from a narcissistic person who only wants you to keep dancing to their tune and won't respect you or your boundaries.

Perhaps you have already separated from or are considering separating from a narcissist. It's best to consider healing and recovery, which is crucial for maintaining your well-being. The last chapters listed strategies to cope in a relationship with a narcissist, some of which include but are not limited to:

1. Self-care

2. Seeking professional help – therapist or a counselor

3. Self-reflection

4. Setting boundaries.

After cutting off from a narcissistic person, you will need to maintain those routines to facilitate what I will call self-rehab, a process of healing your mental health.

Yet, it's not limited to the points I listed out. You will need some more strategies to heal and shield yourself from a future narcissist. Before progressing to the other necessary steps, I want you to understand that setting boundaries isn't limited to when you are already in a relationship with a narcissist: it starts by you saying NO to any manipulation of any kind, from whomever it may be, whether a total stranger, family members, or friends. Boundaries are like a line or a barrier that someone else cannot cross, and you can't deal with other people, be it a narcissist or not, without it. It's really essential, and that is why throughout this book, we have talked about it more than once. Now let us go over these other strategies.

1. *Establishing Support Networks*: Surround yourself with understanding and sympathetic friends, family members, or support groups that can validate your feelings and offer emotional support.

2. *Letting Go of Guilt*: Let go of any sentiments of guilt or self-blame over the relationship's result. Recognise that you are not to blame for the narcissist's behaviour, and concentrate on moving ahead constructively.

3. *Setting Realistic Expectations*: don't forget that recovery from narcissistic abuse takes time and may include setbacks. Be patient with yourself and have reasonable expectations for your recovery.

4. *Embracing Personal Growth*: Make the most of the experience by learning about yourself and growing as a

person. Identify areas for self-improvement and strive to become the best version of yourself.

5. *Forgive Yourself*: Show self-compassion and forgiveness for any perceived flaws or shortcomings in the relationship. Recognise that you did your best with the knowledge and resources available at the time.

6. *Moving Forward*: Focus on creating a full and meaningful life outside of the narcissistic relationship. Set new goals, build healthy relationships, and seize new possibilities for growth and satisfaction.

Building Self-Esteem and Confidence Following Narcissistic Abuse

Healing from narcissistic abuse requires restoring self-esteem and confidence. This entails acknowledging your worth and value as an individual, regardless of whatever negative signals you may have gotten from the narcissist. It's about restoring your self-esteem and learning to believe in your talents and qualities again.

Cultivating Healthy Relationships and Moving Forward with Resilience

Moving on from a narcissistic relationship requires building healthy relationships based on mutual respect, trust, and support to build resilience. It's about surrounding yourself with people that encourage and inspire you, not tear you down. Building resilience is also important because it allows you to recover from setbacks and confront future difficulties with strength and resolve. You may have a successful and meaningful life free of narcissistic abuse by cultivating healthy connections and embracing resilience.

CONCLUSION

In conclusion, navigating relationships with narcissists is undoubtedly challenging, but it's not insurmountable. Throughout this journey, we've explored various strategies, from setting boundaries to practicing self-care, from cultivating healthy relationships to seeking professional help.

We've delved into the complexities of narcissistic behaviour, understanding its spectrum, and recognizing its impact on our well-being. We've discussed the importance of self-awareness, assertive communication, and resilience in the face of manipulation and emotional abuse.

But above all, we've emphasized the power of self-love and self-compassion. Healing from narcissistic abuse requires courage, strength, and a commitment to prioritize our own mental and emotional health.

As you embark on this journey of healing and recovery, please remember that you are not alone. You have the support of loved ones, friends, therapists, and a community of survivors who understand your struggles and champion your resilience.

May you continue to nurture your inner strength, cultivate meaningful connections, and reclaim your sense of self-worth. And may you never forget that your journey towards healing is a testament to your courage and your unwavering commitment to living a life of authenticity, empowerment, and boundless possibility.

THE END